Horses and Ponies

Horse and Pony Competitions

Marion Curry

GARETH**STEVENS**
GS
PUBLISHING
A Member of the VRC Media Family of Companies

Please visit our Web site at: **www.garethstevens.com**
For a free color catalog describing Gareth Stevens Publishing's list of high-quality
books and multimedia programs, call 1-800-542-2595 (USA) or 1-800-387-3178 (Canada).
Gareth Stevens Publishing's fax: (414) 332-3567.

Library of Congress Cataloging-in-Publication Data

Curry, Marion, 1954-
   Horse and pony competitions / by Marion Curry. — North American ed.
     p. cm. — (Horses and ponies)
   Includes bibliographical references and index.
   ISBN-10: 0-8368-6834-X — ISBN-13: 978-0-8368-6834-0 (lib. bdg.)
   1. Horse sports—Juvenile literature. I. Title.
SF294.23.C87   2007
798—dc22   2006002857

This North American edition first published in 2007 by
Gareth Stevens Publishing
A Member of the WRC Media Family of Companies
330 West Olive Street, Suite 100
Milwaukee, WI 53212 USA

This U.S. edition copyright © 2007 by Gareth Stevens, Inc.
Original edition copyright © 2004 by Miles Kelly Publishing.
First published in 2004 by Miles Kelly Publishing Ltd., Bardfield Centre,
Great Bardfield, Essex, U.K., CM7 4SL.

Gareth Stevens managing editor: Valerie J. Weber
Gareth Stevens editor: Leifa Butrick
Gareth Stevens art director: Tammy West
Gareth Stevens designer: Kami M. Strunsee
Gareth Stevens production: Jessica Morris

Picture credits: p. 5 for Williams Trailers Ltd; p. 7 (top) Shires Equestrian Products;
p. 7 (bottom) (Lingjohn Juniper) Nipna Stud; pp. 20, 28 © Bob Langrish. All other images
from Miles Kelly Archives, Corel, digitalvision, DigitalSTOCK, and PhotoDisc.

Printed in the United States of America

1 2 3 4 5 6 7 8 9 10 09 08 07 06

★ *Cover Caption* ★
Competition horses can learn surprising tricks. This horse and rider are going down an extremely steep hill.

Table of Contents

Words that appear in the glossary are printed in
boldface type the first time they appear in the text.

Horse Shows

* Horse shows give horse owners a chance to put their animals in competition with other similar horses and **ponies**.

* Riding stables and other groups offer lessons on how to show horses.

* Showing a horse takes a lot of planning. First, owners must choose shows where their horses' abilities can be judged accurately. Then owners must send in applications and entry fees and find a way to take their horses to the show.

* To make sure horses will look their best, horse owners **groom** their horses thoroughly the day before the show. They also clean and polish their **tack**.

Handlers lead their horses around the ring at **inhand** showing classes. Horses do not wear saddles for this competition.

* On the morning of a show, a horse needs to be fed and groomed again. Owners can also braid the horse's mane and tail and prepare the horse for traveling.

* Owners must remember to pack the horse's feed, water, grooming kits, first-aid kits, and tack. They need to pack clothing for the riders as well.

* The owner who starts to get ready early will have plenty of time to load the animal calmly and have a relaxed drive to the event.

* Owners should report to the show secretary on arrival and collect the animal's show number. Sometimes show schedules change during the weeks or months of planning.

* Before going into the ring, horses need light exercise to work off excess energy.

On arriving at the show ground, owners should unload their horses and allow them to stretch their legs and become used to the surroundings.

* **Dressage** (dreh-SAHGE) lets a horse and rider show that they work together well and that the horse will obey exact orders.

* For dressage, a horse and rider go through a series of tests in a large arena or open field. A judge pays attention to how a horse moves, how it behaves, and how suitable it is for the job it will do. A horse's appearance is also very important in dressage. The judge awards points based on these factors.

* Riders signal their horses with their hands, feet, or legs. These movements tell the horses what to do. If a horse ignores the rider's signals, it will lose points in the competition.

* Horses also lose points in dressage by using the wrong **gait** — **trotting** when they should be **cantering**, for example. Sometimes horses

An advanced dressage rider, wearing top hat and tails, shows how smoothly the horse can move.

lose impulsion, which means they use their front legs instead of their back legs as their source of power. Horses also lose points if their rhythm is wrong.

★ In some show classes, or competitions, owners do not ride their horses but lead them around the ring in front of a judge. These contests are called inhand or halter classes. When the owner rides the horse, the class is called ridden show.

★ In ridden show classes, riders show their horses singly as well as in groups.

★ A good show horse must be well-behaved. It must not disobey its rider or show any anger toward other animals.

★ Turn out, or the overall appearance of the mane and tail, is also important in dressage. Braiding a horse's mane often shows off a good head and neck.

Ponies do not have their manes or tails braided or trimmed for the show ring. They appear in their natural state.

Show Jumping

★ Show jumping competitions usually match the **competitors** according to age and experience. Novice classes are for new riders. Green horse classes are for horses that have just started training.

★ Show jumping includes individual jumping competitions and events for pairs and teams. Sometimes horse and rider wear costumes.

A show jumping arena contains a set of colored jumps.

- Before a competition begins, the riders may walk the course on foot to memorize it and figure out where they should get into position to take the jumps.

- Horses lose points if they knock down a jump, refuse to make one, or take too long to jump. Their mistakes are called faults. If a horse refuses to jump a fence twice, it is out of the competition.

- The riders who manage to go through the course without any faults qualify for a second round of jumping. This round is a timed, shorter course over higher jumps. The winner is the one with the fewest faults and best time.

- Jumps may be *uprights* — straight up-and-down fences — or *spreads*. Spreads have two sets of uprights, creating a

> ★ *Fascinating Fact* ★
>
> Powerful show jumpers can jump more than 7 feet (2.13 meters) high.

broader jump. If a horse bumps any fence, the fence falls.

- A course often includes turns and combination fences. Double and triple fences, for example, stand closer together than other jumps. It is important to approach them at the correct angle and speed.

- Some courses include water jumps — either broad waterways with low fences in front or ditches followed by higher fences. A horse that puts a foot in the water, is given faults.

- A good show jumping horse is brave, quick, and **agile**. It also listens to the rider.

Horse Racing

★ Horse racing is a worldwide sport. One of the most popular racing events is over flat ground on a course that varies from 3/4 mile to 2 miles (1.2 to 3.2 kilometers). **Thoroughbreds** are the favorite racing **breed**.

★ Horse racing became popular during the eighteenth and nineteenth centuries. The British Derby started in 1780 and the British Grand National in 1839.

★ The Kentucky Derby is the most famous horse race in the United States. It began in 1875.

The Curragh is the headquarters of flat racing in Ireland. It can trace its history back to the third century and **chariot** racing. There are no jumps in flat racing.

Racehorses begin races in starting stalls. These gates prevent horses from starting early.

★ Steeplechases were originally races from one church steeple to another. Horses had to jump any fences that were between the two churches.

★ Before cars and trucks were invented, racehorses had to walk to the racetrack. They often had to leave home weeks before the race began so they had time to recover from their journeys.

★ **Jockeys** race in "silks" — colored hats and blouses. The color identifies the horse's owner.

★ Many people consider Man O' War the greatest Thoroughbred racing horse ever. He set many world records and was the biggest money maker of his time. One season, it was almost impossible to find any other horses to run in the races because everyone knew that Man O' War would win.

★ *Fascinating Fact* ★

The Dubai World Cup race in the United Arab Emirates has the biggest cash prize in the world — $6 million.

Cross-Country and Eventing

★ Riders need to be very fit to complete a cross-country course, but courses exist for all kinds of riders, from beginner to advanced. Cross-country jumps are fixed objects, such as stone walls. They call for great bravery from both horse and rider.

★ If competitors take the wrong course, fall off twice, or refuse a jump three times, they will be taken out of the race.

★ A horse and rider have to complete a cross-country course within a set time. They receive penalties for falls and refusals.

★ Jumps are spread out. Riders have to pay attention to the condition of the ground to get the best from their horses.

This horse and rider bravely jump a cross-country fence in water.

* Before competing, riders get a chance to walk the courses and study the jumps to figure out the best way to approach them.

* In one-day or three-day events, the different kinds of rides are spread out over time. Riders compete in dressage, show jumping, and cross-country rides as well as track and steeplechase rides. The horse with the fewest penalty points at the end of the event wins.

* Event horses have to be at least five years old to compete.

* Some events are for teams or pairs.

* The dressage test aims to show that a brave horse capable of show jumping and cross-country rides is also calm and well-behaved.

* Road and track events do not involve jumps. They test trotting and cantering ability. The steeplechase races involve jumping fences made of brush.

Jumping in and out of water requires a bold horse. To be successful in cross-country events, a horse and rider need to trust each other.

Harness Racing

* ★ Harness racing is one of the most popular **equestrian** sports in the world.
* ★ There are two different gaits or types of harness-racing horse: the pace horse and the trotting horse.

Harness-racing drivers wear safety helmets and goggles to protect themselves.

Pacers usually wear **hobbles** to prevent them from breaking their gait.

★ The pace horse moves its right front and back legs at the same time. Then it moves its left front and back legs.

★ In contrast, the trotting horse moves its legs in diagonal pairs. Its front and rear legs on opposite sides move forward together.

★ If a horse breaks out of its correct gait, the driver must pull over to the outside of the racetrack. This penalty makes him lose ground to the other racers.

★ The horse pulls a sulky — a lightweight two-wheeled cart.

★ In harness racing, a movable starting gate ensures a fair start for all competitors.

★ In Switzerland, harness-racing horses pull sulky sleighs on a snow-covered track.

★ Horses often wear thick nose bands called shadow rolls. These bands limit the horses' views of the ground and prevent them from being scared of shadows.

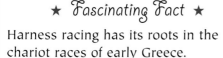

★ *Fascinating Fact* ★

Harness racing has its roots in the chariot races of early Greece.

Western Riding

* Cowboys in the United States developed **western** riding during the nineteenth century, but it has become popular worldwide.

* Western riders usually do not wear protective headgear. They usually wear Stetson hats, shirts, riding **chaps** (worn over pants), and gloves. Riders may also wear decorated leather cowboy boots that extend well above the ankles.

* Western riders shift their weight and pull the **reins** on

This horse is wearing a typical western bridle and saddle kept in place with a breastplate. The rider wears a Stetson hat, chaps, and cowboy boots.

their horses' necks to control their speed and direction.

★ By holding the reins in one hand, western-style riders have one hand free. Riders can hold ropes in their other hand to catch livestock.

★ Riders carefully learn the tricks of reining. At shows, riders go through sets of movements, including turns and circles. They earn points for perfect moves and well-behaved horses.

★ On dismounting, a western-style rider removes his or her right foot from the **stirrup**, swings it over the saddle, and then steps down with the right leg first. In English-style riding, both legs come out of the stirrups before riders dismount.

★ Western riding has its own names for a horse's gait. The canter is called a lope and the trot is known as a jog.

The sign of the western cowboy, the Stetson protects him from the sun, the wind, and the rain.

★ *Fascinating Fact* ★

The Stetson was named after John Batterson Stetson, the man who made the first cowboy hat.

★ Trail riding for fun is a big part of western riding.

★ **Rodeo** developed out of western riding. Rodeo events include saddle-**bronc** riding, **bareback**-bronc riding, and bull riding. Timed events include roping and barrel racing.

Rodeo

- ★ The first rodeo was held in Arizona in 1888.

- ★ The first rodeo rules were created in the 1930s when the Rodeo Association of America (RAA) and the Cowboys Turtle Association (CTA) started.

- ★ Rodeos include six basic events: barrel racing, calf roping, steer wrestling, saddle-bronc, bareback, and bull riding. Winners take home large cash prizes, but rodeo riding is a very dangerous sport, and riders often get hurt.

- ★ In **bucking** competitions, riders only have to stay

This western display team shows the precision and skill of the western horse and rider.

on the rearing animals for eight or ten seconds, but they often do not make it.

- ★ In calf roping, riders have to **lasso** calves while riding their horses, tie their ropes to their saddles, dismount, and tie the calves' legs together.

Barrel racing competitions go fast, and contestants lose points for knocking over a barrel.

★ A steer is a young bull. The rider in steer wrestling is called a bull dogger. These riders leap from their horses, grab a steer's head, and wrestle it to the ground. A second cowboy, called a hazer, keeps the steer from running away from the bull dogger.

★ Barrel racing is an exciting timed competition in which horses race around three barrels in a cloverleaf pattern.

★ Riders go very fast in reining competitions. The horse and rider must work closely together while performing particular movements. In the sliding stop, a horse runs at full **gallop** and then sits down on its rear legs and slides to a stop.

★ Rodeo horses have to learn to make quick turns. They have to learn to pivot — to make a quarter turn on their back legs after stopping.

Endurance Riding

★ The Western States Trail Ride, or Tevis Cup, is a one-day, 100-mile (160-km) ride in California. It is the oldest modern-day **endurance** ride. It began in 1955 and has been held every year since then.

★ The horse's condition is very important in endurance riding. Riders can be taken out of endurance rides if **veterinarians** think they are hurting their horses.

★ The motto of endurance riding is "To finish is to win."

★ There are different kinds of endurance rides. Some are races, and all the riders start at the same

Endurance riding requires a strong bond between the horse and rider. Spending time training the horse helps build this connection.

time. Some endurance rides are simply for fun or to train riders. Sometimes a ride must be finished within a certain time limit. Other rides are just for riders with certain kinds of experience. Rides may be 20 miles (30 km) long or as many as 100 miles (160 km) long.

★ For some shorter rides, any fit horse can enter a contest. Although Arabian horses often are the best at long-distance riding, other breeds also do well on 20-mile (30-km) rides.

★ Before taking part in a ride, a horse must have a **farrier** check its feet and shoes. It will also have to go to a vet who will check its heart rate and make sure the horse is in good condition. The vet will also check for injuries.

★ Along the ride, riders present themselves to officials at checkpoints. Riders also need a back-up crew. These friends meet them along route, cool down the horses by rubbing them down with water, and give both the horses and the riders drinks of water. Longer rides include vet checks.

★ On finishing a competitive ride, a rider must report back to the vet within a set time to present his or her horse for examination again. Riders earn ribbons for completing rides and for bringing their horses back in good condition.

Mounted Games

★ Mounted games or **gymkhanas** (jim-KAH-nas) are fun for everyone who takes part — from parents who lead children on ponies to competitive teenagers. These games are played on ponies because riders usually need to reach objects on the ground.

★ The word *gymkhana* comes from India, where people have played mounted games for hundreds of years.

★ Small children usually lead their ponies across the game field. Older children ride during their games.

The pony and rider need to have a good sense of balance. In the flag race, the rider has to lean over to grab the flag while moving and turning quickly.

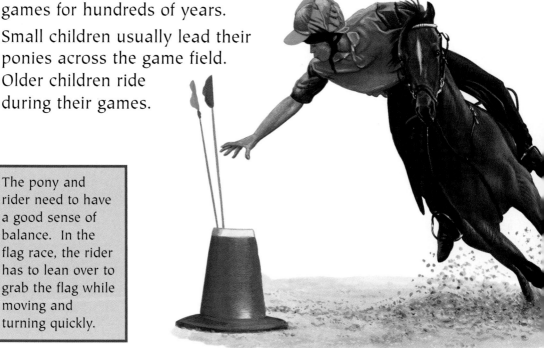

- ★ Many games are relay races with four people on each team. Each rider must ride or lead his or her pony through a short course and accomplish some task in the middle before the next rider takes over. The task could be dropping a tennis ball in a bucket, breaking a balloon with a lance, carrying a bucket full of eggs at the end of a pole, walking through a hula hoop, or weaving through a line of bending poles.

- ★ A calm pony is good for games, but it must also be fast-moving and able to stop suddenly. The good gymkhana rider is well-balanced, stable, and able to get on and off a pony easily.

- ★ Riders should make sure their ponies are not afraid of flapping flags or other race equipment and that they are happy to run alongside the riders during race activities.

- ★ No whips or spurs are allowed in the games. Riders should wear safety hats, **jodhpurs**, and riding boots. Body protectors, or foam-filled vests, are optional.

- ★ First, second, and third places in each event win points and badges made of ribbons. The overall champion wins a trophy.

- ★ In the United States, the Pony Club runs mounted games competitions with regional and championship finals.

- ★ Each year, the United States Pony Club selects a team of riders to participate in an international competition among riders from Great Britain, Canada, and Australia.

Polo

* British **cavalry** officers serving in India in the nineteenth century introduced polo to Europe and the Americas.
* A fast team sport, polo is now played worldwide.

Polo riders wear special helmets, protective knee pads, and boots. Their ponies wear leg and tail protection.

- ★ In polo, two teams of four riders try to score goals by hitting a ball through goal posts with a polo stick. The polo stick is called a mallet.

- ★ The polo ball is difficult to hit, because it is only 3 inches (8 centimeters) in diameter. While the ball used to be made of wood, it is now usually plastic.

- ★ The game is divided into timed sections called chukkas. The ponies get some time to rest between plays.

- ★ Each rider may ride more than one pony in the course of a polo game.

- ★ A trained polo pony is worth a great deal of money. It must be fast and agile, able to stop instantly from a gallop and take off again quickly.

- ★ Polo ponies learn to turn while running fast.

- ★ The best ponies come from Argentina or from the Southwest or the Rocky Mountains in the United States.

★ *Fascinating Fact* ★

The word *polo* originates from the Tibetan word *pulu* meaning "ball."

Polo ponies are actually horses. Players originally used ponies because the players need to reach the ball on the ground. Now they ride horses.

Olympic Games

★ The 1900 Olympics included competitions for the best equestrian long jump and high jump. These events were dropped from the Olympics shortly afterward, however.

★ Three-day **eventing** and dressage were added to show jumping in 1912. Individual and team events are held today in all three sports.

> To compete in the Olympics, horses and riders must be the same nationality. They also must have experience in top international competitions.

- ★ Horses must be at least seven years old to take part in the Olympic Games.

- ★ Riders from France, Germany, Brazil, the Netherlands, and Great Britain won gold medals in equestrian events at the 2004 Olympics in Athens.

- ★ Riding events are the only Olympic competitions where men and women compete equally. When the modern Olympics began, however, only male riders who were officers in the cavalry could take part in the three-day event.

- ★ Women were allowed to compete in Olympic dressage for the first time in 1952.

- ★ Liselott Linsenhoff was the first woman to win a gold medal in an equestrian event. She was part the German dressage team in 1968. In 1972, she was the first woman to win Olympic gold in the individual dressage.

- ★ Lis Hartel of Denmark won a silver medal in dressage in 1952 and 1956 in spite of having to be helped on and off her horse. She had been paralyzed by polio in 1944.

Show jumping was the first equestrian sport in the modern Olympic games. It was introduced in 1900.

★ Vaulting is doing gymnastics on a moving horse.

★ The American Vaulting Association sponsors many competitions. It also runs programs that use vaulting to help people with special needs. These people may be blind or have lost parts of their bodies. The sport helps develop coordination.

★ Most vaulters do their tricks while their horses are cantering. Difficult tricks, however, are often performed when the horses are walking.

Team vaulting competitions involve riders carrying out six or more basic exercises. They get a grade for how well they perform.

- For centuries, British riders have hunted foxes for sport. In 2005, Great Britain banned fox hunting because it was a **blood sport**. A new sport, drag hunting, has taken its place.

- Drag hunting does not involve killing an animal. Hounds and horseback riders follow an artificial scent pulled over the ground by a human runner.

- The hunters still jump walls, fences, and streams in their fields. The hunt ends when the dogs catch up with the person dragging the scent.

- Horseball is a popular game in parts of western Europe. It could be described as a cross between basketball and rugby.

- Horseball is played on horseback on a field about 225 feet (70 m) long using a ball with six leather handles.

The object is make three passes to teammates and then shoot the ball through a hoop.

- A fast-growing sport, Le Trec started in France in the 1970s. The name stands for *Technique de Randonnee Equestre de Competition,* which means "competition of equestrian excursion techniques."

- Riders first follow a detailed map and cover a route in a limited time. Then the riders show their control of their horses, trying for the fastest walk and the slowest canter. Finally, riders must complete certain tasks on an obstacle course, such as opening and closing a gate, jumping a log, or going down a steep slope.

Glossary

agile: able to move and turn quickly

bareback: without a saddle

blood sport: a sport in which an animal is killed

breed: group related by common ancestors

bridles: horses' headgear that includes the bit, mouthpiece, and reins

bronc: an unbroken, or untrained, horse

bucking: springing into the air with its back arched

cantering: quickly running with a three-beat rhythm that is slower than a gallop

cavalry: soldiers on horseback

chaps: leather leggings worn over trousers

chariot: a two-wheeled battle car

competitor: a person or animal that takes part in a contest

dressage: an event in which a horse moves precisely by following orders

endurance: the ability to put up with hardship

equestrian: relating to horseback riding

eventing: the three equestrian sports — dressage, cross-country, and show jumping

farrier: someone who shoes horses

gait: a way of moving on foot

gallop: a fast run

groom: clean and brush

gymkhanas: games played on horseback

hobbles: bands that tie a horse's legs loosely together

inhand: led by straps on a horse's head

jockeys: people who are paid to ride horses in racing events

jodhpurs: riding pants

lasso: catch with a long rope that has a noose at the end

multiple sclerosis: a serious muscle disease

ponies: small horses, less than 14.2 hands high (57 inches tall)

reins: straps a rider uses to direct a horse

rodeo: a show of western riding skills

steer: a young bull that has been neutered

stirrups: a pair of small rings attached to the saddle for a rider's feet

tack: horse equipment such as saddles and bridles

Thoroughbreds: a breed of horse that is especially good at racing

trotting: walking moderately fast

veterinarians: animal doctors

western: a riding style that uses a western saddle for trail riding and rodeo events

For More Information
Books

First Riding Lessons. Riding Club (series). Sandy Ransford (Kingfisher)
Galloping across the USA: Horses in American Life. Transportation in America
    (series). Martin W. Sandler (Oxford University Press)
Horse Showing for Kids : Training, Grooming, Trailering, Apparel, Tack, Competing,
    Sportsmanship. Cheryl Kimball (Storey Publishing)
Joining the Rodeo. Rodeo Discovery Library (series). Tex McLeese (Rourke Press)
Jumping. The Horse Library (series) Betty Bolte (Chelsea House Publications)

Web Sites

Gymkhana Game
www.abc.net.au/rollercoaster/saddle/interact/game/default.htm
An interactive game site that is fun and informative.

Horse-country.com
www.horse-country.com/aindex.html
Twenty-eight great activities including coloring pages, mazes, word scrambles,
and crossword puzzles

Washington International Horse Show
www.wihs.org/home/index.cfm
Event information, pictures of last year's winners, news

Publisher's note to educators and parents: Our editors have carefully reviewed these
Web sites to ensure that they are suitable for children. Many Web sites change frequently,
however, and we cannot guarantee that a site's future contents will continue to meet our
high standards of quality and educational value. Be advised that children should be closely
supervised whenever they access the Internet.

Index